THE STRATEGETICS
PRACTICAL & CONCISE
MODELS FOR THE LEADER

ERIC ROEMER

ISBN: 9798402362208

For those who have gone ahead,
may we honor the lessons
and legecy you've left.
And for those who follow after,
may we keep the path clear
and stay out of the passing lane.

CONTENTS

THE STRATEGETICS
Section One: The Leader

LEADERSHIP   POTENTIAL   GROWTH   FOCUS   MAINTAIN & SUSTAIN

INTRODUCTION

In the late 1970's and early 1980's, a young leader working at the headquarters for a small denominational American church began to think about how to better develop leadership skills in young people. Keith Drury started thinking about leadership before it became its own section in bookstores. He wasn't doing it to make a name for himself, sell books, or pack out conference halls. He wanted people to have the skills to be better and do better.

Drury began to collect all the best models and lessons he was hearing and reading about leading effectively. He would pull them out of books, meetings, teachings, and anywhere else they might be found. He started thinking of lessons he'd learned himself. He arranged them into a grid with little pictures or words and called them Strategetics.

Once the models were collected and arranged, he invited a small group of young pastors together. Many of these young leaders were right out of college and just starting out. He taught them the Strategetics and then sent them back to the churches and organizations they were serving. He would follow up with them and check in on how their work was going. He continued to collect, create and arrange more models. A year later, he called the young leaders together again, added some new young leaders to the group, and taught them the updated version. He then sent them back to where they were working. This process repeated for five or six years. Then, Keith Drury took a job as a professor and stopped working on the Strategetics.

That group of young leaders didn't stop using them. Over the last 40 years, the people who were part of the group have become some of the most effective, innovative and insightful leaders in the country. They have grown amazing organizations, affected culture, and trained others to do the same. They even passed the principles of the Strategetics on to other teachers who have built leadership training emperies.

Keith Drury was one of my professors twenty years after the Strategetics were laid to rest. Little glimpses of some of these models showed up in his lectures. They were powerful and stuck with me. After a decade of being in ministry and leadership, my tank was running empty. It seemed like there were more things I didn't know than I did. So, I went to get coffee with a retired pastor to learn anything I could. During the conversation, I mentioned one of the lessons I'd learned in Dr. Drury's classes. This older pastor got excited and asked, "You know about the Strategetics?"

I did not. I had never heard that word before. I was fairly certain he was mispronouncing something. But he wasn't. He had been part of that original group and began to tell how it had made all the difference in the success he'd had over his career. I was interested.

I emailed Keith Drury that afternoon. He emailed me some images from scanned materials he'd made forty years before and a few recordings that had been done. He'd never written any of it down. It was all taught in lectures. I didn't really understand what I was looking at. I emailed him back and we decided to get breakfast.

We met at a diner next to the university where he had taught. We sat across from each other in a booth and Dr. Drury lectured for almost 4 hours. I was inspired, amazed and heartbroken. Heartbroken because this insight was exactly what I had needed in my early career, but it's time had passed. It was sitting, mostly forgotten, in a file on his hard-drive. All but a small group of exceptional leaders approaching retirement had never even heard the Strategetics.

Keith Drury agreed to let me share it with whomever I could. He just told me not to give him any credit, but he deserves credit. Dr. Drury has spent his lifetime making other people better without seeking any credit along the way. He is a great and humble man. He said the Strategetics are just a "briefcase" he filled with things he'd learned from other people. I have shared these principles and models with other leaders, other professionals, and my own staff. Everyone has responded the same way I did: they wished they had learned these things sooner.

I have reorganized, updated, cropped and added to the Strategetics. This is a curated collection of models and principles that have served as kernels to most of the leadership material produced over the last forty years. However, this is only part of the collection. There are many more models and principles, and the system will continue to develop.

Each of these Strategetics are intended to help you understand your role as a leader, reach your full potential, grow and develop, be focused and intentional, and maintain and sustain your effectiveness for a long time. They should help you see that shifting your perspectives and expectations will allow you to become a better, more effective and inspiring leader to those people that may follow you.

Individually, these are simple and concise bits of insight, but when combined together, they become a philosophy for purpose and success. Knowing a philosophy and living by it are not the same thing. Applied knowledge becomes wisdom, and our organizations, businesses, churches and world are in desperate need of a new generation of wise leaders.

THE STRATEGETICS
Section One: The Leader

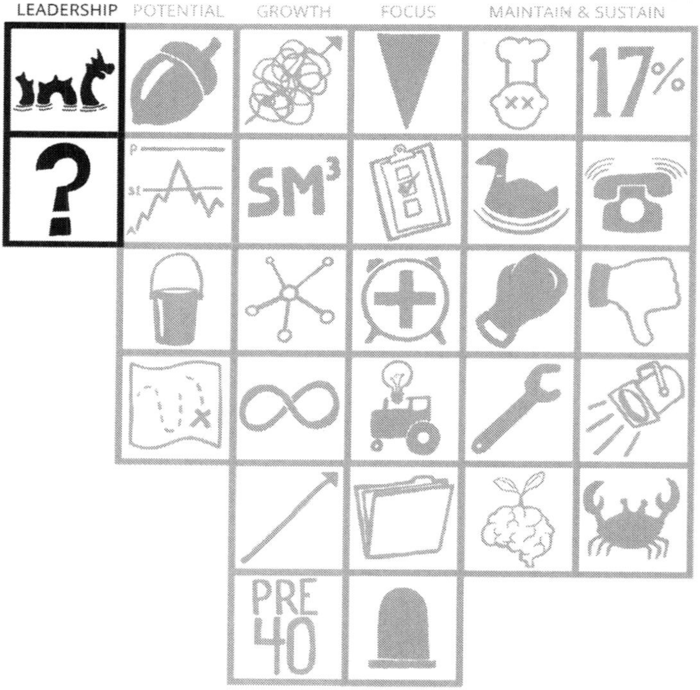

PART ONE: **LEADERSHIP**

DRAGONS

The first model is all about Risk. Leadership is all about risk. Leaders are people who choose to risk and create the confidence and conviction needed to get others to join them in that risk.

Think about the great explorers who chose to push the boundaries of what was already known, what had already been done, and where people had already gone. They looked at the maps that other people made and saw at the edges there were pictures of sea monsters. Warnings were written in Old English, "There be dragons."

Most people would say, "Okay, I'm not going there then." But the leader is the person that says, "Let's go find out", and inspires a crew of people to go with them.

If the maps said, "There is treasure or riches" on the edges, everyone would want to go. It takes a leader to get people to move into the unknown. It takes a leader who is willing to risk looking a dragon in the eyes to convince others it is worth coming along for that journey.

The question you have to answer as leader is first whether or not you are willing to look a dragon in the eyes. If the answer is no, if you aren't ready to risk, then you probably aren't ready to lead yet. But, you can become a leader by deciding to do what it takes to get ready. You can decide to become the kind of person you need to be. You can decide to do the things that need to be done. The rest of these Strategetics are all about you becoming that leader, and developing the ways of thinking needed to take your crew out to meet those dragons.

The second question you have to answer is what dragons you're going after. Where are you leading people? Is it starting a new business, a new project or a new ministry? Is it a new organization, team or church, or is it a dramatic change in the direction of an existing organization, team or church? You need to be able to look at the map and see the direction you need to move. Which edge of the map are you willing to risk whatever it takes to go for? Which edge of the map are you so convinced needs to be conquered that you'll be ready to influence others to join you?

There are dragons out there. If you are willing, you can become the person that will go and find those dragons and get other people excited enough to join you on that journey. That's what leadership is all about. This is what leaders do.

WHY

There are plenty of different reasons people choose to become leaders. The specifics of those choices set the trajectory towards leadership and what type of leaders those people will become.

There is no one motivation that is right for all people to become leaders. But focusing on the lesser aspects and byproducts of being a leader usually creates a ceiling of possibility and opportunity for aspiring leaders.

Leaders are usually honored by receiving more influence, respect and authority in our society. Great leaders even become fixtures in our history books. These things happen, but they should not be our primary motivation for wanting to lead. These things are all inward focused, so setting our trajectory on them will ultimately keep us from the bigger vision and potential you have to make a difference and inspire other people to follow us.

So, why should you try to lead then? What should your motivation be?

You need to be faithful to the calling you feel deep inside of yourselves or the responsibility required of you by others as you pursue becoming a leader. Your motivation to lead must be bigger than you. It may be an idea, process or product that you know needs brought to market because of what it can accomplish in and for other people. It may be independence and an opportunity for a better life for your family and community. It may be the necessity to make wrong things right, broken things work and bad things better.

Influence, respect, authority, money and history books might come along too, but they can't be the point. Those are the byproducts of leadership but they should never be the goal.

PART TWO: **POTENTIAL**

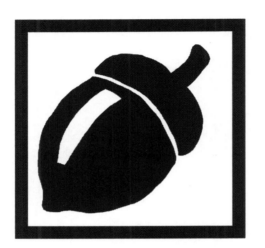

ACORN

The acorn is not a new model for the capacity and potential in leadership. It is so well known and often used to illustrate the potential for great things that are in each of us that it has almost become cliché. It has gotten this status honestly though, because it is a good model with plenty of truth that you must not miss.

A mentor gave me an actual acorn twenty years ago when they shared this model with me. I've kept it in a box with other significant things I've collected over the years. Every once in a while I will stumble across it and remember the lesson, but I also remember how easy it is to miss the point.

See the irony? That acorn, with all its potential has stayed in that box for twenty years to teach me about all the potential that I have too. Potential doesn't make leading happen. Potential doesn't get leadership done. Potential doesn't grow the tree.

Releasing that potential, cultivating that potential and investing that potential makes for an effective leader.

It is true that inside every acorn is a mighty oak tree and a forest of mighty oak trees and many forests of mighty oak trees. But the twenty-year-old acorn in my box hasn't grown anything... because it hasn't gotten dirty. It hasn't put in any time in the summer heat or the winter frost. It has just stayed safe and clean in a box.

It isn't enough to know that you have great potential. You do have great potential. Everyone does! What matters is what you do with that potential. How you are unleashing, cultivating and investing your potential to lead is what matters. This should be the real lesson of the acorn.

SELF-IMAGE

One of the major obstacles to realizing and experiencing all the potential that you have to lead and make a difference is our own self-image. Henry Ford said, "Whether you think you can or think you can't, you're right." What you believe about yourself and your abilities becomes a ceiling for your reality.

Most often, you base what you believe about your potential on your past achievements. You allow what you have done to set the baseline for what you will do. This becomes a trap that limits you from seeking to do what needs done.

Sometimes your past achievements fall short of the bar of self-image you have set for yourself. When this happens, you either beat yourself up for dropping the ball, you explain it away as having an off day, or you find someone to blame for your failure. Any of those excuses may be true.

Sometimes your past achievements have exceeded your bar of self-image. When this happens you believe you got lucky. This is the trap of self-image: instead of expecting great things in the future, you give luck all the credit and you don't aim that high again.

You need to learn to raise the bar of self-image as close as possible to your true ceiling of potential. You need to make your true ceiling of potential the target you aim for and expect from yourself. When you do that, others will begin to expect that from you too and will be more willing to join you in what you choose to do as you lead.

Think about the last time you got "lucky" and surprised yourself. Now imagine if that became your new baseline of self-image and expectation. Stop selling yourself short. Stop holding yourself back. Find out what you're really capable of and how high your ceiling really is.

MIND PAIL

You have to starting thinking about yourself differently to raise your self-image. This model is all about changing your thinking.

Imagine that your mind is a pail, or a bucket, and the way you think is the water inside of that bucket.

The good and positive thinking is hot and warm water. Believing in yourself, trusting the potential is there waiting to grow when you go to work, believing the journey you are taking people on is important and knowing that you are able to lead them on that journey is all hot and warm water.

The bad and negative thinking is cold water. Thinking you aren't good enough, your best accomplishments were just luck, your passion won't make sense to anyone else, and no one would ever want to follow you is all cold water.

To change the way you think and raise the bar of your self-image you must change the temperature of your bucket. This means you have to control what you let go in your bucket. First, stop letting other people pour cold water into your bucket. Stop letting other people throw ice cubes into your bucket. If you surround yourself with people that can tell you all the reasons you can't do something and can't be something, your bucket will get colder, and your bar of self-image will get lower. Constructive criticism and wise counsel are important, but there is a difference between that and people that are chilling your mind pail.

Don't give other people an opportunity to lower your temperature. When they do, be quick to warm it back up. Also, watch that you don't throw cold water into your own bucket. If you have made a habit of tearing yourself down before other people get a chance to, then you might be the one pouring in the cold water. If you have convinced yourself that you can't before you even try, then you might be the one throwing in the ice cubes.

CHANGE. Change the way you look at yourself. Change the way you think about yourself. Change the way you talk to yourself.

Make a list of all the things about yourself that you know are good and true and all the things you want to be true about you. Actually write it out. Start with "I" statements and always frame them in the positive. "I am a creative person." "I am a hard worker." "I have important things to share." Write it down. Don't be weird, but find ways to tell other people about it. Hang that list up in places where you will see it and read it often. Do it over and over again. This is adding warm water and hot coals to your own bucket. Do it every day until the temperature is where it needs to be.

Find other people who believe in you and encourage you. Surround yourself with people who are generous with hot water for your bucket, and learn to be generous in giving hot water to others. Break off relationships and limit time with people that only make you colder. Take care of your mind pail so you will have what you need to reach your potential and accomplish your greatest goals.

LEVELS OF LIVING

A man is walking down the street and comes to a construction site. Brick masons are working on the other side of the fence, and the man calls over to the first one and asks, "What are you doing?" and he answers, "I'm laying bricks."

The man walks a little farther and comes to a second brick mason and asks, "What are you doing?" and he answers, "I'm building a wall."

The man walks a little farther and comes to a third brick mason and asks, "What are you doing?" and he answers, "I'm building a great cathedral so generations to comewill have a place to gather, and celebrate and wonder at the majesty of God, the universe and everything in it."

All three men answered the same question honestly. They were all doing the same thing and they were all doing different things. It wasn't their activity that made their answers different; it was the way in which they understood their capacity and the potential of what they were accomplishing.

People can live similar lives but experience totally different things all because of the level of living in which they are choosing to engage. For this model there are four levels: role, vision, mission, and quest.

Role:

The lowest level of living is for acorns in boxes, low-bar self-image people holding buckets of ice cold water who are just stacking one brick on top of the other. These people live to fill a role assigned to them by someone else. They play the part that is expected of them and not much else.

Vision:

The second level of living is when you see what could be and what should be but is not yet. It is a pile of bricks that could be a wall if everything falls into place. People living the vision level of life have allowed themselves to wonder and dream about their own potential but haven't taken the steps toward making that vision anything more than a dream. They believe there is potential in the acorn, but they haven't gotten their hands dirty putting it in the ground.

Mission:

The third level of living is when work is getting done and people are being lead. Potential is being tapped into. A higher self-image is being realized. The warm water from a full bucket is starting to overflow out into the world. People living on this level have a defined purpose, direction, and cause that they are focused on and affecting. They can tell you their mission. If it is a big enough mission, they are probably leading others to accomplish it with them… but this isn't the highest level of living there is.

Quest:

The top level of living is about giving your whole life and being to the adventure to which you have been called. It is more than just something to accomplish. A quest is a fire in the bones. No matter what it takes or what you encounter along the way, a quest must be finished. Even if it means sailing to the end of a map and staring a dragon in the face, there is no quitting or reason to abandon the call.

A person living on mission can convince others to join them through explanation and become their leader. A person living out their quest draws others to themself without even trying. They are oak trees. They have lost sight of their own self-image and only see the ceiling of potential above them. Their buckets are boiling over. People beg to follow people living out their quest.

LEADERSHIP   POTENTIAL   GROWTH   FOCUS   MAINTAIN & SUSTAIN

PART THREE: **GROWTH**

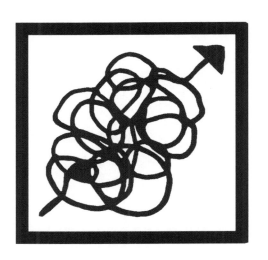

COMPLEXITY

Growing into your potential as a leader requires a balanced understanding between the complexity of leadership and the simplicity of leading individual people. Complex things need to be treated as complex things should. Simple things need to be treated as simple things should. Cross those paths and both your growth as a leader and the things you are trying to accomplish will collapse.

J. Robert Clinton wrote in *The Making of a Leader*, "The factors in success of a leader are more complex than meets the eye." Outside forces are working around you. You must understand there is a complicated web of factors that is influencing your success or failure.

The timing of the endeavor in which you are leading people into is one of these complexities. You've heard people say that an idea was "before its time," and that's why it didn't work out. Your idea, program, team or organization might be before its time too. You cannot control this complexity.

Other people are another one of these complexities. The followers on your team and the competitors that are working against you both have a great deal of influence over whether you fail or succeed in what you are setting out to do. You cannot control other people.

Current events are a third complexity that will have an impact on your work. A recession, a fire, a market disruption or even a global pandemic are all things that are outside of your control but will directly influence whether you are a success or a failure as you lead.

You must acknowledge the complexity of factors leading to your success or failure to grow as a healthy and effective leader reaching your full potential. You must understand that you cannot take success or failure too personally. There is so much more to the equation than just you.

Learn to control the things you can. Do the things you can to grow. But don't blame yourself for things outside of your control. Personally taking on the weight of all the complexity around you will keep you from becoming the leader you should be.

SELF-MADE MAN MYTH

While you should not blame or credit yourself for the complex factors affecting your success or failure from the outside, neither should you ignore the potential those complexities have to help you grow and develop.

Many would-be leaders have bought into an unhealthy myth that true success is being a self-made man or a lone genius. These leaders believe the lies of pride and selfishness; claiming there are a few exceptional people who can kept their heads down, ignore the others and work harder than everyone else until they prove they are the best... all on their own.

Even though that myth is widely held, it isn't how things work. There is no such thing as a self-made man. People have been investing in you and teaching you lessons your entire life. Some of those investments and lessons were teaching you what you could be and do. Other lessons were showing you what you should not become or do. Don't take any of those lessons, investments or relationships for granted.

You had parents, teachers, bosses, co-workers, pastors, coaches and other significant people in your life that modeled different methods and tactics of leadership. All those things, good and bad, have shaped you. All those things should continue to shape you. Pay attention to them.

Your employees and followers will help you become a better leader. Pay attention to them because they will show you the right ways and wrong ways to lead and influence. Your customers and clients will show you the right ways and wrong ways to serve and engage. Your competitors will show you what you are missing and what you could do better.

Pay attention to all of these people. You aren't going to be a self-made man or a lone genius. You need them. Let them make you a better leader. Let them help you grow.

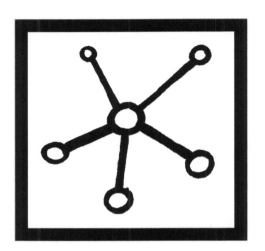

NETWORK

Be intentional about building relationships that will help you grow and develop as a leader. Don't wait for growth to happen, go out and make it happen. Build a network of supply lines to feed your growth and keep that network flowing.

There are three parts to an effective network: above you, beside you and below you.

Above You:
Find people that know what you need to know. Find people that are doing, or have done the things that you want to do. These people might be historical figures that you can only meet in books, so go find them in those books and study what they've done and how they did it. These people might be alive but not interested in building a mentoring relationship with you. Study them and learn from them anyway.

There are other people that you can build a relationship with who are willing and ready to share all their lessons with you if you would just ask. Too many people never take the time to ask. Ask everyone, even the people you think would never take the time to talk with you because you might be surprised.

I regularly call, email, and message authors I'm reading and speakers I've heard to ask questions and try to start discussions. I didn't always do this. I used to think, "They won't respond," and "I'm no one important." I was wrong. Close to 75% of the people I reach out to respond to questions and engage in conversation. Some of conversations have led to meetings, and some of those meetings have led to mentoring relationships.

In sales, an average Lead Conversion Rate (the number of people that buy your product or service compared to the number of people that don't) is around 10%. A great Lead Conversion Rate in a strong niche market can be around 30%. Building a network is all about selling your potential growth. You are asking investors to invest in you. If you ask 10 great leaders to talk and one of them responds, you are winning. So go ask 100 until you get so good at it, they all want to talk. There is an old proverb, "A single conversation with a wise man is better than ten years of study." Keep asking until you get those conversations.

Beside You:
You have friends and peers that should be part of your network. The people beside you can and should be helping you grow, even if they don't realize it. Your peers and co-workers are doing the same things you are. Watch them, talk to them, and learn from them. Even if they are working for a competitor doesn't mean they are your opponent when it comes to building your network. Don't miss out on their work and the ways it can benefit your growth.

Your friends are an important part of your network and the growth it should be causing. Don't be too busy to develop, maintain and enjoy friendships. Too many young leaders get so preoccupied with their mission that they don't have time for friends. This keeps them from growing and developing in the long run. Your friends don't have to do what you do. You need the diversity of experience, insight, creativity, support and downtime to remember that you are more than just the work you are doing right now.

Below You:

There should also be people below you in the network. Employees and followers matter to your growth and development as a leader. You should intentionally matter to their growth and development too. Pay attention to their questions and the ways they stumble, and you can learn more about yourself and the areas in which you need to develop to lead them better. Take time to teach others the lessons you have learned and are learning. The process of teaching reinforces the concepts in your own life and will speed up your development.

Build your network. This isn't a network of contacts and sales leads that you might be able to tap into at some point in the future. This is a network that is about helping you grow and develop. Let it supply what you need to grow and develop as a leader. Time spent getting you closer to reaching your full potential is always time well spent.

THE INFINITE GAME

In the book, *Finite and Infinite Games*, Dr. James Carse added to the field of game theory by making an important distinction between the types of games people play. Not all games are the same. The way you play different games should not be the same either.

A finite game has a beginning and an end. This is like a game of football or baseball. The game starts; there are rules to follow and a set amount of time to follow them. When the time runs out and the game is over, there is a winner and a loser. Someone playing a finite game plays to win.

An infinite game does not have a beginning or an end. The game is s bigger than just winning and losing. The infinite game is about discovery, creativity and growth. Love, business, and politics are infinite games. You cannot win or lose infinite games. You may win a date, a deal or an election, but the game is not over when this happens. It will keep going long after you aren't around to play it anymore. The point of an infinite game is not to win, but to play and get other people to play as well.

Leadership is not a finite game. This Strategetic needs to teach us that you aren't leading to win. You are leading to participate in the discovering, creating and growing that comes in leading. You need to lead like infinite players, always seeking to make the game bigger and include more players in it.

If your only focus is on setting a goal and winning that goal, then what comes next? Another goal? And then another? How long will others keep following you if you keep changing the goal posts?

If you play in order to discover, create and grow, then there is no end. You can keep discovering, creating and growing, and lead others to do the same. You don't have to worry about one failure ruining you or one success defining you. You get to keep playing.

Being an infinite player means you must focus on process of leading. Being an infinite player means you have to get rid of the assumptions and expectations that winning is all that matters. Otherwise, you lose all credibility to lead the first time you lose.

In order to grow and develop, you need some wins and some losses; they are part of the game. You need to have some days where you excel and some days when you fall behind, because you grow through both those days.

Shift your paradigm from thinking that one day you will arrive, win and have everything all figured out. That day doesn't happen. Instead, develop a mindset that you can discover, create and grow every day. Play the game that makes you a better player.

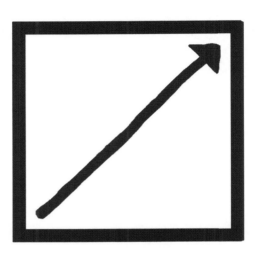

SIMPLICITY

Growing into your potential as a leader requires a balanced understanding between the complexity of leadership and the simplicity of leading individual people. There are so many complex factors that come into play in leading, building, creating, and developing businesses, organizations and causes. A good leader is not someone who adds more complexity to the situations they face. A good leader is someone who can make the complex concepts and situations simple.

Growing as a leader means understanding, embracing and spreading simplicity. It has to start with you as the leader though. You only have so much focus and energy during your time in the game. Don't spend it on complex, wasteful and distracting things and systems.

Decision fatigue is a real thing. Just making the most basic choices every day can drain you physically and mentally and leave you no energy to lead. This is why some of the most productive people wear the same outfit, eat the same lunch, and have the same routine every day. Effective leaders simplify their lives in order to give everything they can to their mission and quest.

There is no need to be fancy and showy in your dress, possessions and behavior. All of that will only become a distraction. Don't become a source of more stress and complexity for yourself or the people that are following you.

If fancy things show up eventually, that is fine. Let them be nothing more than a naturally occurring by-product of success, but do not chase and seek them. Instead, chase and seek growth and development.

Learn the secret to contentment; to enjoy things without having to possess them. Too many leaders have their first taste of success and immediately get preoccupied with the by-products. Bank accounts and property do not mean you are growing and successful, but they can mean you are distracted and becoming ineffective.

Keep focusing on the simple things that will make you better and more able to lead. Keep focusing on the relationships with the people you can learn from, live with and lead. Keep focusing on discovering, creating and growing. Meet the complexities of leadership with the simplicity of a person realizing their full potential.

PRE-40

Growth requires you to be intentional. You have to decide to grow through self-evaluation, building your network and shifting your perspective about what type of game you are playing. You have to make stuff happen.

Growth always takes time. You cannot speed up time, but by having a plan and posture to develop, you can speed up growth. Andrew Carnegie's plan was to spend the first third of his life getting all the education he could, the second third making all the money he could and the final third giving away all he could. He was intentional about using his time to grow before everything else.

Keith Drury said, "Most contributions in your life will occur after you are 40." 40 might not represent the first third of life, but it does seem to be an important marker between developing and delivering. You should still expect to grow after 40, and you should expect to discover and create some things before 40. A good Pre-40 Plan can make that pivot more effective.

For effective growth there should be 10 major components to your Pre-40 Plan.

1.Choose your Life's Wedge: We will address this in the next section.

2.Learn your Trade: You have to take time to develop the actual and practical skills you need to work and lead. Invest yourself in education. You will not regret knowing too much or being too prepared.

3.Learn to Delegate: Learn to work with and trust people. If you don't learn to delegate by the time you are 40, you will never need to learn to delegate because no one will give you the chance. Leaders need be able to let other people do the work.

4.Settle your Personal Image: It is okay for young people to be finding themselves. It is normal for young people to be discovering who they are and deciding how they want to be perceived by others. By 40, you want to have moved past this part of development; know who you are so others will know who they are following.

5.Establish Life Habits: Create order, balance and processes that work for you. Find your flow between creating, leading and living. It will not get easier to establish these things as opportunity and responsibilities are realized, so take care of them early.

6.Order You Family Life: Too many people put off family and relationships until they get the business or organization going. Too many people don't realize that an ordered family life is a huge benefit to growth as a person and a leader. Nothing will bring you better perspective about complexity, simplicity and the infinite game than family. Neglecting family will always turn into a liability.

7.Learn your Strengths: Find out what you are good at and own your strengths. Know what you can bring to the table.

8.Learn your Weaknesses: Find out what you aren't good at and own your weaknesses. Know what you cannot bring to the table and find others who can.

9.Pick your Lifestyle: This is part of simplicity. Don't put the cart before the horse and try to live like a success before you are one. Don't forget about your mission and quest to make a difference because you can buy stuff. Don't get distracted from becoming an infinite player because of shiny trophies.

10.Establish your Network: Do it. Write some emails. Make some calls. Talk to your Peers. Pour into others. This matters.

LEADERSHIP	POTENTIAL	GROWTH	FOCUS	MAINTAIN & SUSTAIN	
			▼		17%
?		SM³			
			⊕		
		∞			
		↗			
		PRE 40			

PART FOUR: **FOCUS**

WEDGE

To grow and lead well you must be intentional and focused. The wedge is a model of intentionality.

If you want to split wood or break through a hard surface, a long and narrow wedge will serve you better than a shallow and wide one. The narrower the angle, the sharper the impact and penetration. The same is true of an effective leader.

You may think you need to know everything in your field, about your market, and be able to do every job in your organization yourself. When leaders think like this it isn't long before they become spread too thin and stop making a helpful difference. You should know as much as you can but become very intentional about what you do with your time and energy.

To really drive deep into the purpose and mission of your business, organization or team, figure out what you are really about. Narrow your wedge to the sharpest angle you can to make the deepest impact. This will save you from unnecessary distractions, becoming spread too thin and losing sight of your real purpose as you try to maintain too broad a focus.

$25,000 PLAN

To have a sharp wedge, be intentional and stay focused, you must develop a system of planning. The model of the $25,000 plan is the story of Ivy Lee and Charles Schwab at Bethlehem Steel.

Schwab bought Bethlehem Steel around the turn of the 20th century, and during those first couple decades, the company expanded rapidly, acquiring many other smaller companies. Schwab knew that rapid growth could kill efficiency by causing the wedge to get too wide and shallow. In 1918, he hired a consultant named Ivy Lee to advise the company on how to stay focused and successful.

Lee went through all the data, interviewed all the managers and executives and came back with the plan. Schwab let Lee meet with each executive in the company to explain a simple organizational method. Lee instructed each executive to spend a little time at the end of each workday to write down the six most important items to accomplish the next day and put them in order starting with the most important. Then, they would start the next day focused on the list until each item was complete, even if something needed to get bumped to the following day. It was a simple plan.

Schwab asked how much Lee expected to get paid for this simple bit of advice. Lee told him to wait and see how it worked for three months and then pay him whatever he thought it was worth. Three months later, Schwab wrote Lee a check for $25,000 (over $450,000 in today's money). This simple plan boosted the company's productivity through intentional focus more than any other plan ever had, and it was taught to every manager and worker in the company.

It was just a to-do list, and it worked to keep the wedge sharp.

You need to have a plan too, and that plan needs to be a system that works for you. But understand that a system like this is more than just setting goals and then getting them done. The purpose of a good system of planning must be to develop a lifestyle of focus and intentionality. Your plan should not just be your task list for the day but a means of developing habits for your lifetime.

The Ivy Lee plan might work for you, or there might be something else. I Bullet Journal with a pen in a paper notebook. Others use apps, sticky notes and all kinds of premade systems. The right system for you is one that works, that you will stick with and that keeps you focused. Find a system that keeps your wedge sharp.

MANUFACTURED TIME

When people consider implementing plans for organization and the ways they need to limit their activity to stay focused and effective, there is usually the same push back: I have too much to do and too little time to do it for this to work for me.

Time is valuable. Time isn't as rare as some people make it sound though. Time is everywhere. You are surrounded by it, and the supply isn't running out. You had time yesterday, and there is going to be more of it tomorrow. It might not feel like there is enough, but that has to do with the way you look at time and not the nature of time.

A scarcity mindset about time can dull your wedge faster than anything else. Change the way you think about your time. If a company needs more widgets to get a project done, they will manufacture more widgets. That company will not complain that they don't have enough widgets and then give up on the project. If you need more time to get a project done, develop a skill, balance your life, take care of yourself or whatever you may be up to, you can manufacture the time you need to get it done.

Don't make up the excuses that there isn't enough. Don't make it so easy to give up. If something is really important, then let it be important. Make the time you need to do the things that need done.

To manufacture widgets, you need to take whatever material widgets are made of, rearrange that material and process it into widgets. To manufacture time requires the resources you have to be rearranged and put to work in the same way. This may mean you have to get up a little earlier or go to bed a little later. This may mean you need to make some trade-offs and spend less time on something else to spend more time on what is important. This may mean you need to cut some things out of your schedule all together.

Time is everywhere. It isn't about how much time you have; it's all about what you do with the time you have. Make time for what you need to get done.

THE IDEA FARM

When you are more focused, intentional and using your time efficiently, you will become more effective and productive. A byproduct of this growth is the production of new ideas. Having new ideas is good and important, but it may also cause problems if you don't have a plan in place to do something with those ideas.

Ideas are valuable. Ideas can and have changed the world. Your ideas are important. Don't lose them for the sake of staying focused and intentional. You will need those ideas to move your organization, team or project to the next level. Have a plan to keep and protect those ideas.

The model of The Idea Farm is all about collecting, protecting and cultivating your ideas. An Idea Farm is a place to keep your ideas and give them time to grow or die. It is important to keep all the ideas on the farm, even the crazy ones that you are 99% sure will die. You might be wrong about them. Don't just throw them away. Give them a chance.

Your Idea Farm should be an actual thing. Don't assume you will remember every idea you think of; it is not possible if you are focused on what you are doing right now. Find a box in which you can throw the ideas written on bits of paper. Have a folder in which to stuff them. Buy a notebook you can carry around that is only used for your Idea Farm. Create a file on your laptop or cell phone.

Plant all your ideas in one place as they come to you and then go back to work. From time to time, go back to check on the farm and revisit the things you've planted. See if anything has grown. See if an idea's time has come. See if you are ready to harvest. Or see if you need to wait a little longer.

The Idea Farm isn't just about cultivating ideas. It is also about cultivating a habit of innovation and creativity. Just because you are focused and intentional doesn't mean you need to develop tunnel vision. A good system and plan must include and require innovation and creativity on a regular basis. Don't limit yourself by not having a plan in place. An Idea Farm is a huge part of a good plan.

THE MOTIVATION FILE

Cultivating creativity and innovation as you grow and expand can be dangerous. Creative people can become extremely negative. If a creative and innovative person is surrounded by things they know should be better but don't have the ability to do anything about them, negativity may take root. Negativity will keep you from accomplishing as much as you could. Negativity will keep you from becoming the leader you could be. Have a plan to redirect negativity into something positive.

Creativity sees what could be but is not yet. Without a plan to address this sort of creativity, creative energy will grow into frustration and criticism. A critical leader demotivates the people around them, losing effectiveness and eventually followers.

The model of The Motivation File is a practical and effective tool to transform negative into positive. Just like The Idea Farm, create an actual file you keep somewhere. This file needs to be a safe place to release and store possible frustrations so they don't get in the way of you being focused on what you can do right now. This is a place to release negative thoughts in a positive way so you can get back to work.

When faced with possible frustration for the way something is being done, use the Motivation File to reframe the situation as a future opportunity. Do this with positive language.

If you have a boss who runs meetings poorly and you know you could lead and communicate better, don't dwell on what is wrong but on what you would like to do better. Always state your comments for the Motivation File in the positive. "I would..." statements turn a negative reality into a positive future opportunity. Make a list titled, "If I were the boss...", and then list the positive "I would" statements below.

"If I were the boss... I would make our team meetings shorter and make sure each person has a opportunity to be heard." Add your statement to the list in The Motivation File. The next time you are frustrated with your boss, add another statement to the list. Store the file away, bury it, and wait for the opportunity to use it if you become the boss one day. You will already have a plan in place to do things better. You will have turned the negative frustrations into a positive plan, without getting bitter and distracted along the way.

Make lists in your Motivation File that may never turn into opportunities just to avoid letting negativity to grow and distract you. Make a list about what you would do if you were ever the President, or if you ever run the coffee shop that keeps getting your order wrong, or if you ever owned the airline that lost your luggage. Make a habit of turning your frustrations about negative situations into innovative and positive opportunities.

LIFE SENTENCE

Neil Armstrong was the first man to walk on the moon. Alexander Graham Bell invented the telephone. Babe Ruth was one of the greatest baseball players of all time. Every one of these men did more than just those things with their lives, but this is how you remember them.

Clare Boothe Luce was an American author and politician in the 20th century. She gave a piece of advice to President Kennedy to encourage him to stay focused on the most important things he had to do with the time he had to do them. She said, "A great man is one sentence."

Like it or not, one sentence is all you get. Our legacy and lifetime will eventually be condensed into a single Life Sentence. This is true for great historical figures. This is true for mentors, family members, and friends that have passed away. This will be true for you.

Living a life of intentionality and focus will give you the opportunity to affect your Life Sentence. Sharpening and maintaining your life's wedge will give you the opportunity to affect your Life Sentence. Finding and keeping a system and plan that develop the habits you need to be successful will give you the opportunity to affect your Life Sentence.

What do you want your Life Sentence to be? Is your life's wedge focused on driving towards that sentence? Is your system and plan working towards that sentence? Are the things you are doing, the way you are using your time, and the focus on your life leading you to that sentence? If the answer is no, then what needs to change to get you there?

Successful and effective leaders are intentionally focused. They have plans that are bigger than just goals. They have plans that will affect the way they are remembered.

PART FIVE: **MAINTAIN & SUSTAIN**

THE STARVING BAKER

The model of the Starving Baker is a story. A baker opened up shop in a small village. He began making bread that the people in the village loved. It was the best bread they had ever had and he began selling out of it every day. The people in the village couldn't get enough of it, so he decided to start making more. The people bought more, and he was still selling out every day.

People from the villages around his village heard about the bread, and they started coming to the shop too. He began making even more bread every day and selling it all. People loved the bread, people loved the baker, and the baker loved the work. It was good he loved what he was doing because he was working all day, every day. The shop was making huge profits. The village became known as the home of the baker. He was a success.

As people came day after day to get the bread, they failed to notice that the baker was changing though. They didn't notice that every day he was a little thinner, a little paler, and a little more hunched over. The bread was still excellent but the baker wasn't. He grew weaker, but he would not stop baking because he was a success. He wasn't about to slow down.

Then, one morning, the Baker's shop wasn't open. A line of people stretched down the street. They were all waiting for their bread. When they couldn't wait any longer, one of the customers broke through the door to see what was taking so long. They found the baker, collapsed and dead, on the floor of the kitchen. They rushed his body to the doctor who determined that he had starved to death.

The baker was working so hard to make all the bread he could, to sell all the bread he could, and become a success that he never stopped to eat. Every day he was surrounded by the best bread there was, but he didn't make time to have any of it. Now he was gone, and no one had any bread. They don't remember him as a success. He was the fool that starved himself to death baking bread.

A great leader who knows why they are leading, is living up to their potential, is growing in their ability, and is focused and intentional in what they do, must take time to maintain and sustain themself. Too many leaders get a taste of success and lose their appetite to live. They become one dimensional. They neglect their purpose, potential and plans. They lose sense of everything that brought them to where they are. They starve to death. Game over.

There are seasons where things have to be lean. There will be times that your work will require more effort than you can sustain for the long haul. Know this going into those seasons, put a time limit on how long you will stay there:. Three months, six months, one year of working harder than you can maintain. At the end, you stop and eat. You rest. You regain your bearings and reevaluate your circumstances. But you don't keep going until you starve.

Set that season in stone. Share it with those people closest to you and have them keep you accountable. No matter the mission or quest, it isn't worth losing yourself. Where will your followers be without a leader? Make maintaining and sustaining yourself a priority for a successful organization, program, or team.

DUCK HUNTING

One of the biggest obstacles to maintaining and sustaining a healthy life in leadership is our perspective. Focusing on personal growth and purpose will help, but there should be more than that. Just like a successful baker has to remember to eat every day, a good leader needs to remember to check their perspective often.

The model of Duck Hunting is all about checking perspective. A hunter goes out early to the pond and spends the day calling, watching and waiting for the ducks to come. When ducks come, he takes his shot. He prepared and planned. He does what he can do when he can do it. He takes his prize and goes home.

He arrives home, and his family asks, "How did the duck hunt go?" He can either answer, "Great. I got three ducks today." or he can say, "It was awful; 97 ducks got away." Both answers are describing the same hunt, but not the same perspective.

Too many leaders develop the second perspective. It is the critical mind. You are taught to push yourself harder. You are taught to settle for nothing less than excellence. You see all the ducks you miss, all the times you've failed, all the flaws and all the ways things didn't work out the way you wanted, but you miss the success. You forget you are succeeding.

No one kills all the ducks. That isn't how duck hunting works. Mallard genocide is the goal of crazy people. Hunters shouldn't be people like this.

There are times when you need the critical mind. I want my surgeon or the lady who cuts my hair to aim for absolute perfection. I don't need them to be okay with missing something. But, I don't expect them to live their entire lives like that. You shouldn't expect that of yourself either.

The hunter that celebrates getting three ducks is our rational mind. The reality of duck hunting has never been to kill them all. A real and rational expectation for yourself should focus on what you can get and not on how you fail. You will have off days because everyone does. You will blow a deal. You will be rude and short. None of that stuff means you're a bad duck hunter.

Too high of expectations for yourself is unsustainable and will take you out of the game. Focusing on your failures and not your successes will lead you to more failure. Let yourself off the hook. Prepare the best you can, aim the best you can, take the best shot you can and enjoy the hunt. You don't have to get them all. Learn to live with missed ducks.

ROPE-A-DOPE

In 1974, Mohammad Ali fought boxing heavy weight champion George Foreman. Ali was a 4-1 underdog. Foreman (25 years old) was bigger, younger and stronger than Ali. Ali (32 years old) was smarter than Foreman.

Ali used a tactic Foreman had never seen. Later, Ali called it the "rope-a-dope." Ali leaned against the ropes, and covered up his head and body with his arms, and let Foreman punch him over and over again. Ali blocked and deflected all the punches he could and threw a jab here and there. Ali mainly just let Foreman punch him. For eight rounds, Ali leaned against the ropes, and Foreman gave him everything he had until he didn't have anything left. When Foreman was out of energy from throwing all those punches, Ali knocked him out and became the champion.

In 1994, 20 years later, George Foreman was 45 years old and beat 26-year-old Michael Moorer to become the Heavyweight Champion again. He did it by letting the young, stronger boxer punch him over and over again for nine rounds. When Moorer had used up all his energy, Foreman knocked him out in the tenth round to win. The rope-a-dope worked again.

The Rope-a-Dope model is to remind us that sometimes you have to take a few punches on the way to success. Sometimes it feels like and looks like you are losing on the way to victory. There is a temptation to fight harder when you start to get hit, but you shouldn't give in to that temptation. Learn to let up a little bit and think about the long game during those times.

Leaning on the ropes means learning to apologize to the people you are working with and leading. Apologize when you have messed up. Learn to admit when you have made a mistake and own it. Don't fight harder than you need to, trying to cover up or ignore your mistakes. Learn to compromise with other people when compromising can be done. Don't punch yourself out always trying to get things just the way you want them.

You aren't retreating or failing. You are maintaining and sustaining your strength while learning how to best overcome the obstacles you are facing. Learn to lean on the ropes and wait for your opening.

PIT STOP

The PIT Stop model stands for Putting In Time. Don't get in a hurry. That can be hard when you feel like you aren't accomplishing what you think you need to. It can be hard not to get in a hurry when you feel like you're getting punched over and over again. You will want to move on and get away from the situation, but sometimes that is the worst thing you can do. Sometimes you need to stop, lean against the ropes, and put in some time.

Everyone gets to a season in life where it doesn't feel like anything is happening. Sometimes it feels like you aren't going anywhere. You may need these times to get ready forthe next leg of your journey though. Do not dread these times, but use them to prepare. Use these times to regain focus and develop a strategy for moving forward. Use this time to gas up your tank, change your tires and maintain and sustain for the long haul.

These are great seasons to reflect on the lessons you have learned from your own past experiences. Use your pit stop to develop your character and become a better person who will then be a better leader. Develop new skills and study new things when life gets slow. When your organization, project or team is moving fast again you won't have the time to grow so do it while you are putting in time and waiting for your mission to pick back up and get moving.

Great leaders will always be more interested in developing themselves than their work. When there is an opportunity for a PIT Stop, take it.

MIND FIELD

As you are maintaining and sustaining, checking your perspective and putting in the time to develop through difficulties, remember to keep your mind safe. Your mind is a field, and what you plant in that field will grow.

If you plant anger, bitterness and negativity in your mind, you will harvest more of the same over time. This can be hard to avoid when faced with failures, getting punched over and over again, and waiting in pit stops when you feel like everything is passing you by. The worst thing you can do is let frustrations allow the anger and negativity to take root. No one wants to follow an angry and bitter leader for long. An angry and bitter leader has nowhere good to lead people.

Don't dwell on the failures, punches and waiting. Rather see the positive opportunities that are always present. Shift your perspective. Learn to cultivate your thoughts into what is good now and can get better.

Plant hope for the future, let it grow, and harvest enough to share with those people following you. Practice gratitude. Get in the habit of identifying the good in yourself, in your circumstances and in the people around you. Doing this allows you to water crops and not the weeds growing in your Mind Field.

It is not enough to focus on your actions and habits alone. Take care of your mind, and pay attention to what you are allowing to grow there.

17%

SEVENTEEN PERCENT

Learning to maintain and sustain yourself through the slow and difficult times will make you a better leader when things get fast and exciting. This is why maintaining and sustaining are keys to excelling as you lead people, projects and organizations.

I have a friend who is a firearms instructor for law enforcement and the SWAT team. He is an expert shooter. He is the best of the best and trains others to be better in situations that matter the most. When he runs the course at the shooting range, he will constantly shoot 100%. Perfect scores every time.

He has explained to me that when they are training on the shooting range there are drills they run that simulate stressful environments. They try to make training situations as difficult as possible so officers will perform well in real times of crisis. My friend is a 100% shooter normally, but during these drills that number drops to 17%. And my friend is one of the best.

The 17% model teaches you that preparing and planning are important, but you must never forget what stress will do to your ability to respond and lead. You should try to prepare for when things will be difficult, anticipate getting punched, and be ready to be forced into a PIT stop. Plan to be ready for these seasons, but don't be surprised when they hit you harder than expected. Real life is the best training program. It is also the hardest. No one gets 100% all the time in real life.

You are not going to be at your best during times of stress and crisis. Don't expect to be. Don't beat yourself up when you only perform at 17%. Prepare, but don't forget about the reality that hard things are going to be hard sometimes. It's okay to hope to do better next time.

THE RINGING PHONE

So far, many of the models for maintaining and sustaining your personal health and balance have had to do with checking the expectations you place on yourself. This model and the next couple are about being aware of the expectations others may try to force on you. Know what they might be and be prepared to handle them in a way that is best for you, your organization, team or project.

The model of The Ringing Phone tells us that just because the phone rings does not mean the call is important or the call is even for you. When you are in the middle of something more important, don't feel obligated to answer.

Too many leaders will sacrifice their own health, focus and balance because of the list of requests and demands that others bring to them. Good leaders learn to silence the phone and let things go.

Stop trying to do everything that people want you to do. Stop telling yourself that you need to do everything they want you to do. It isn't true. If it needs done, you are probably not the only one that can do it. So if you are working on something else important, let them call the next person on the list.

Learn to delegate actively and passively. Allow other people the opportunity to get involved by creating an atmosphere where everything doesn't rest on your shoulders. This will mean letting go of some control over how things get done. Become okay with letting go of some control. You will be able to maintain and sustain better because of it.

COMPETENCE FAILURE TRAP

The Competence Failure Trap is a warning. Work gravitates to a competent person until that person fails, and then the opportunities stop coming. This is an important reason not to answer every phone call and take on more than you are able to handle.

This is how the trap works: You do well at the task you are doing, and people notice. They offer you opportunities to do more; you take them, and do well at them too. More opportunities come, and you keep excelling until you pass your ability level. Then, you fail and people think you are unreliable. You plateau and end up stuck in a place where you cannot excel.

I've seen great salesmen who love their jobs get promoted to managers who aren't very good at managing and end up hating what they do. I've seen great college professors leave their classrooms and students to become unfulfilled, mediocre administrators.

Remember to stay focused on the mission and quest. The goal is not to make it to the top of the ladder but to make it to the top of your potential. The goal is to make the greatest difference leading others to reach their potential as well. Learn to say no to opportunities that don't match your mission and abilities.

THE ENCORE PROBLEM

Another expectation that others can force on you and throw you off balance is The Encore Problem. This is like The Competence Failure Trap but without a promotion or new opportunity.

Competence always tries to beat its own record. You always try to outdo yourself but too often end up just beating yourself up. You make a great deal or give an amazing presentation and feel like you are right at the top of the ceiling of your potential. When you go to prepare the next deal or plan the next presentation, you become overwhelmed with the fear of not doing better or even as well. Others begin to expect every next move to be better than the one before.

The expectations get too big. Carrying those expectations takes more energy than you have to do the work. You feel like you have to give them an encore every show that will blow them away. That is unrealistic and unsustainable. Stop thinking like that.

Don't let your own success cripple you. Enjoy it. Learn from it. Move on. When you get to a big enough win that you know there is no encore for, it is time to change the show. Change your goals as a leader. Change the structure and flow of the organization. Change your definition of success. Change as a leader.

If you don't meet The Encore Problem with change, you are committing yourself to getting stuck in a rut. You become a slave to your expectations. Your expectations will beat you up. Change your expectations before they get a chance.

You don't owe them an encore every show. When the time comes, walk off the stage and go write a brand new song instead.

CRAB BUCKET

Others may have an expectation that you should not and will not succeed. Whatever their motivation behind this may be, it is important to be aware that there are going to be some people that will try to stop you.

The Crab Bucket model is all about being aware of the people that want to keep you from reaching your potential. If you put one crab in a bucket, it will be able to crawl and claw its way out of the bucket and back to freedom. But if you put two or more crabs in a bucket none will be making it back to freedom. As one crab begins to get higher up on the wall of the bucket, the other crabs will reach up and pull it back down, try to crawl on top of it, or even break its legs.

All people aren't like this. Every person who pushes back as you lead is not trying to destroy you either. But there are some people that are. Be aware of this. Learn to identify the people that are trying to help you with constructive criticism and concern and the people that are out to stop you from succeeding. Do what you can to learn from the former and distance yourself from the latter.

Sometimes crab-people will actively and intentionally seek to sabotage you. Others just have a mentality that seeks to keep everyone around them low with them. These crab-people tend to be negative about any change, opportunity or even success. These crab-people usually dislike and distrust anyone in any leadership position. The crab-people seek to find their joy in not feeling joy.

It is best to avoid these crab-people if you can. Remove them from your team or move them out of your organization if you can. If you cannot, be conscious that they are crab-people and treat them accordingly. Don't take their criticism personally or seriously. Don't seek comradery in getting negative with them about anything. Don't criticize other leaders in their presence. Don't try to pull them back down if they start to climb and succeed either.

Maintain and sustain what you know is right and best for you. Demonstrate the models that work to them. Hope they shed their shell and decide to change. If you've been a crab-person; own it, admit it and be done with it.

THE STRATEGETICS
Section One: The Leader

CONCLUSION

Our world is in desperate need of wise leaders. So much leadership material is focused on the process of leading instead of developing wisdom in the leader though. These Strategetics are focused on developing that wisdom.

Wisdom comes from choosing to shift perspectives from what is most common to what is most beneficial. Shortcuts to influencing other people and gaining power are common among people who desire positions of leadership, but they are not beneficial. Those shortcuts are not benefiting the leader, organizations, missions, or the world we share.

Wise and good leadership must begin with a clear and healthy understanding of the role and purpose of the leader. You must understand that your potential to fulfill that role and purpose is achievable. When you have an unhealthy and incorrect view of who you should be as a leader and why you are leading, you miss out on developing innate potential. Then, the teams, programs, and organizations you lead miss out on fulfilling their greatest mission.

To achieve your potential requires a commitment to growth, focused and intentional behavior, and a life-style of building habits and perspectives that will maintain and sustain balanced and wise leadership. This is the purpose of each of the Stratgetics in this book. Individually, each model is only a bit of insight. Combined, they become a framework for wisdom and a road map to successful leadership.

As you reflect and study these models, notice how often the principles will show up in your daily activity as you interact and lead. When you engage with other leadership material, be aware of how often the kernels of the Strategetics show up in what is being taught. Be generous with these models, share the principles and point out the truths that you have found here. This will reinforce the Strategetics in your development and cause those around you to grow as well.

Our organizations, businesses, churches and world are in desperate need of a new generation of wise leaders. Use these Strategetics to become those wise leaders and to develop others to join you.

- NOTES -

- NOTES -

Made in United States
Orlando, FL
29 January 2022